EXCHANGE

Chris Drury

Kay Syrad

EXCHANGE

act of reciprocal giving and receiving

give: bestow, allot, grant, commit, devote, entrust, hold

receive: admit, welcome, accept, recover,
pick up, take hold of, take in

FOREWORD

The way our complex societies have evolved over the past two hundred years has given us a truly rich civilisation. The climate change challenge is now demanding that we drop our dependency on burning fossil fuels for energy and that we treat the natural biodiversity systems of our planet with care and respect. The food we eat and the legacy of its production is central to this notion of care.

Three farms in Sydling St Nicholas and Godmanstone in Dorset have radically changed their approach to food production and the farming of the land. It is a salient story, and the sculptor Chris Drury and writer Kay Syrad have embedded themselves into the lives of these farms to witness how change happens and why. EXCHANGE is their artwork that has been two years in the making.

Eighteen months ago Chris Drury buried one hundred sheets of art paper deep into the soil of the farm of Chris Legg in Sydling St Nicholas, and over time it collected a history of the minerals and microbiome of the earth as it was farmed. He then surveyed the plant diversity of a cubit of land from the uplands of the farm. The natural drawings collected here are a visualisation of that process. Meanwhile, Kay recorded conversations, asked the farmers to write, created poetry and, with great skill, crafted a collective narrative which witnesses what it is to be a farmer. It narrates why they have developed a practice that encompasses how we can care for our habitat and produce food that is harmonious with our own metabolisms. A simple, undeniable record of care.

For the past fifteen years Cape Farewell has focused the creative energy and vision of over three hundred artists and creatives, asking them to embrace the challenge of climate change. From working with climate scientists in the High Arctic and headwaters of the Amazon to the island communities of the Scottish Islands, they have produced a cultural outpouring that witnesses our civilisation's greatest challenge: climate change and how we arrived in the age of the Anthropocene.

This book is the equivalent of 'slow art', a carefully evolved work created by artists in conversation with the farmers and the landscape. I extend my heartfelt thanks to the generosity of those who have made this narrative possible: Will and Pam Best of Manor Farm, Chris and Suzanne Legg of Dollens Farm and John and S-J Morris of Huish Farm.

David Buckland, 2015
Artist and director of Cape Farewell

Open the gate, know how wood yields, how metal resists. Step over the threshold, to encounter a ley field violet-blue with chicory flowers; or walk hard over starve-acre grassland; remain humble before the tall corn easing in the wind (*across the talking corn she goes*). Admire the ancient wheat, Maris Widgeon, sown both for bread and thatch; the kale and spring barley, leaves of clover big as lily pads, stubble fields, fallow fields, margins of quinoa and heathers for the bees; skylarks, wheatears, mistle thrushes, song thrushes, two ring ouzels, seagulls and terns after the plough and a little flock of linnets. Apprehend hedges, copse, gorse (its scent as sweet as coconut), ditch, folds, pens, yards, electric fencing, stables, paddock, stores, a chalk barn (each block scored with labourers' lines or letters) and the cow stalls cleared that summer's day for the farmers' wedding.

At twilight, scoop up or sink down into a dusty slippery mound of grain in the barn; in the morning, ride on a shining blue tractor, a 'mule' or a jump-started Kubota. Follow the path and track, the Rights of Way and rites of passage. Navigate the grassy ridges and furrows of the old water meadows, an unreliable bridge over the rivulet; find a well, vat, tank, water boatmen in a trough once cleaned by goldfish, pond, stream, the old two-stone watermill. Go in and out of the thatched farmhouses, cottages ruined or not, towards tarpaulin-covered ricks, a shepherd's caravan, a lean-to, a long bath, see the sheep, cows, bulls, horses, roe deer, badgers, foxes, chickens, dogs, rats, birds, dragonflies, grasshoppers and the sky, halfway up.

THREE FARMS

Manor Farm, Godmanstone

Huish Farm & Dollens Farm,

Sydling St Nicholas

Dorset

Godmanstone, Godmerston, Godmiston, Godmynstone or Godmarineston, lies on the river, or rivulet, of Cerne, within the dominion of the chalk-hill figure, the Cerne Abbas Giant. *Godman's ton* may have a post-Conquest origin like Forston or Herrison further downstream. The area is thought to have been assessed under the name *Cernel* in the Domesday Book and by 1000 AD the village was well established, with a church (now Holy Trinity with its four rare bells founded in 1607 by William Warre of Leigh), a mill, orchards and gardens, probably a forge, with livestock producing meat, eggs and milk, wool, and wheat for bread and barley for ale in times when the '*corn was threshed with flails, and winnowed by tossing it in the air for the wind to blow away the chaff.*'

Cross the road from Manor Farm to Mill Plot (a watermill for the corn), see the Victorian water meadows and Gore Mead (Old English *gara*, or *gar*, a spear; here, a triangular meadow formed by the road on one side and the river on the other). Back over the road into Tim's Field and Hunter's Plot with the majestic oaks, Coates Ground (barley stubble) and the fine old barn; Church and Higher Fields, Wether Close (*wether*, a castrated ram) and Ram's Plot next to the wood, and if you look through the leaves or over the stile you can just see the new bell tower down by Bushes Barn on Huish land.

Or chase up through the calving paddock behind the farmhouse with *the sun that walks his Airy Way* and on through Bottom, Middle and Top Pigeons Closes (ley, wheat or barley) up to the tumulus in Eweleaze (*henleaze, cowleaze*) left into Red Acres (new ley following oats), stooks and hay ricks and young pigs squealing in the top barn. Then down the Down to North Field, which like Higher Field has the best soil and hedges shaped into a long 'S' so that ox ploughs could turn more easily on the headland, or up and right to Six Acre. Below, Green Avelands (perhaps *Averlands* after Æthelflæd in 921 AD), and Coney Gree, once owned by the Coniger family or maybe it comes from the twelfth-century Anglo-French, *conil*, for a long-eared rabbit.

Bring the cows down in morning mist or dark, walk alongside them, close, urging, repeating go on, gu' aarn. Pat and nudge the cows until you can close the gate to the yard. In the milking shed, study the teats, tweak the teats, smooth the udders, spray, wipe, pat, rub, hold to attach a cluster of electronic pumps. Try to dodge the shit of waiting cows. Get whacked by the pumps swinging back into place. Hose the cow shit off rubber apron, stalls and cows. Train three calves to suck from rubber teats in the barn. Fill three plastic bottles with colostrum for the orphan calves. Thank the two nanny heifers with seven charges between them. Rinse, pour, upturn, shake, hose. Sloosh down the bulk tank room. Talk to the parson, who arrives on a bicycle, about plans to sell the herd and about the poet-farmer Wendell Berry, who meanders *into the peace of wild things.*

Revive a birthing heifer with a large spoonful of liquid Arnica, watch the new calf's efforts to stand up within minutes, how the mother nudges him over and tucks him under her chin to finish licking him. Select homeopathic remedies for other ailments: retained placenta, mastitis, bee stings, coughs, husk or hoof, bruises of the sole (soul) using *The Herdsman's Introduction to Homeopathy* written by your own herdsman, Philip Hansford, and Tony Pinkus – but first of all, know your cow, fuss and nurse your cow, and don't have too many cows. Study glossy AI catalogues from the USA and select for the best Holstein-Friesians, for the finest, strongest, healthiest dairy herd, then struggle with the electronic Kingshay Dairy Manager with its calendrical lists and definitions of lameness and accommodate the Locomotion Scorer whilst observing with your own eyes the way each cow walks away from the milking shed.

Advise on the making of stooks and hayricks for a new film of *Far from the Madding Crowd*, fall in love with Carey Mulligan as Bathsheba just like you fell in love with Julie Christie in 1967. Not many years later, provide organic bottled milk for Unigate in an early pilot scheme, end up supplying every branch of Waitrose and Safeway from Penzance to Inverness and operating as the only commercial organic dairy farm in Dorset for ten years, whilst raising three children. Then complete the annual Herd Health Management Plan, navigate relations with the Soil Association, the Rural Payments Agency, the Environmental Health Agency, the Farm Assurance Scheme, the Food Standards Agency for Raw Milk, and the RSPCA, who ask that the cows be supplied at once with a two-brush scratching post in the yard.

Each cow is breathing, each cow,
And the field is breathing
In a south-westerly wind this day
Where what seems grass is moss,
Gametophyte or matted stems
To hold a reaching blade
Of Vernal Grass, tapered – so
Sweet-scented – and at last
A flawless clover heart. Maybe
Early hair grass and this one's
Six-splay architecture cries its
Clutch of ink-drawn seed pods,
Dried out Burnet Saxifrage in tiny
Fronded fists – while
Each cow selects a grass, wraps,
Tugs it with its tongue.

"I became puzzled about the need to spread something 'artificial' on the land to encourage the growth of plants, and also wondered if it was really necessary to apply sprays to crops to prevent the diseases and pests that the salesmen for these products assured us would come our way. It seemed to me that Nature must have its own answers to these problems, and through observation and experimentation we began to find ways to work with the forces and energy of Nature to grow healthy crops and thus maintain good health in our stock. In so doing we could try and avoid causing the damage to human health, especially in children, that seemed to be resulting from exposure to these new products, most obviously the pesticides. We searched for ways to farm without chemical inputs. After a time we found that we were not alone in this development, and that we were beginning to farm in what was called an organic way."

Pam Best, Manor Farm

In English, there is no one word to describe a woman whose life is bound up in the work of a farm, only 'farmer's wife', 'woman farmer', 'country woman'. In Latin, a farmer's wife is *agricola uxorem*, a female farmer in Spanish is *agricoltora* and in French, *une fermière*, whilst a female dairy farmer is une *productrice de lait*. In fact the word 'dairy' comes from the old English for maid, a woman employed in a house or farm, a dairy maid, a *dey*.

"The wife of a farmer is at times a farmer in her own right and at other times she is the 'farmer's wife'– in fact during each day she is juggling her time between these two calls and probably many others – likewise the *he* farmer is at times being a farmer and at other times being the husband of the other farmer – there is the partnership, but somehow the term 'farmer's wife' seems to belittle the roles of the she farmer. One thing is for sure, farmers seem to need a lot of looking after. Well, I must sort out the kitchen and then to bed."

Pam Best, Manor Farm

Lay a Dorset hedge, starting at the top, laying uphill, hedge behind you and the plashers laid flat because the hedges round here are planted on banks. Next, rid out the brambles, ivy, elder, old man's beard, honeysuckle, dead wood and plants rooted outside the hedge line, and see what you have (thorn, hazel, ash, holly). With a thin hedge, trim the side branches and cut upright stems at an angle very close to the ground about three-quarters of the way through and lay them down along the hedge line using a chainsaw, axe, bow saw or billhook. With a thick hedge, cut out the thick stems and have them for firewood, disentangle the uprights, reach up and cut out the side branches, leaving enough to make a stockproof barrier. Visualise how each stem will look when it comes down, plan where to lay it – beside, on top of, or entwined with those already laid. Anchor down to ensure it looks solid and flowing and use pegs (*kippers*) made from hazel or thorn offcuts to drive in and hold the plashers down and in, and make hoops to tuck into the lowest plashers on each side and pull tightly over the hedge. When you meet a tree (ash saplings mainly, or elm, oak, holly or beech), leave it to grow into a tree unless the hedge is thin. Finally take a sharp hook or lopper and nip off any bits sticking up or out. Tidy up, take what you need for stakes or the boiler and burn the rest when it's dry.

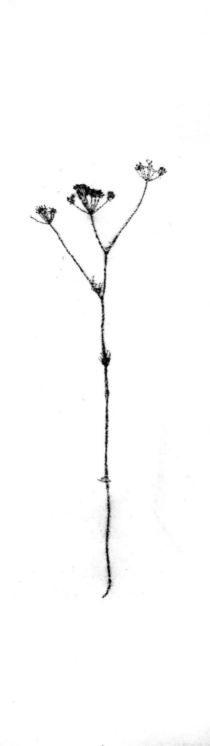

Reap, bind, stook, haul, thresh, flail, truss, winnow and comb, by hand, for nearly a thousand years, until the small steam-powered threshing machines were set up in the barns. Despite the 'Captain Swing' riots, Luddites and the Tolpuddle Martyrs in West Dorset, more and larger machines came in, with rotating drums to thresh the corn against a concave mesh, a further separation and winnowing through sieves, and straw walkers with a fan blowing wind through them. *The thresher is a machine which certainly holds the attention. Like a clear thought or a solved riddle, it looks perfectly obvious.* Later the mechanical reed comber was fitted on top of the threshing machine, and for harvesting came the horse-drawn reaper, cutting the stems and leaving rows of cut corn for the binders, and later a buncher to drop just the right amount of corn for the binders to make the sheaves. Then the knotter, a three-horse reaper-binder which cut the crop and dropped it in rows of sheaves already tied with sisal twine. The wheat destined for thatch still has to be cut by these old binders and pulled by small tractors, and the sheaves still have to be stooked, ricked and later fed into the reed comber, here on Manor Farm.

This and previous page adapted from descriptions given by Will Best; quotation from John Stewart Collis

"Cows are like collie dogs, but a bit lazier. On the whole they are full of kindness and generosity. You can't punish a collie, only encourage her, and to a large extent the same is true of cows. Gentleness, kindness and patience are needed in the herdsperson, together with an ability to make it clear to the cow what it is you want her to do, and make it easy for her to do it. You must remember that her hearing and sense of smell are better than her sight, so she will recognise you largely by your smell and voice: hence the importance of talking to her, and of raising your voice to call her and lowering it to drive her. As to assessing the intelligence of cows – usually when we complain of cows being stupid it is us who are being unintelligent."

Will Best, Manor Farm

The essence of the farm

Land Landscape Harmony Fields Trees Hedges
Birds Birdsong Creatures Plants Fruits Flowers
Man and Produce Silence (almost) Cattle
The sound of cattle in the distance

Respect for animals for farmers for the
earthworm insects birds for the soil

Responsibility to care for the land for future
generations to produce good food
to share, like the poster:

*'The Earth is a garden
and we are the caretakers'*

Pam Best, Manor Farm

"I have realised, more and more, that the impulse in my work is the impulse of local adaptation, which puts the burden squarely on my own life.

It is understood that nonhuman creatures adapt to their places or they don't live . . . But for humans it's not just a biological process. It's a process that involves us entirely: our imagination, sympathy, affection, our local culture and conversation, local memory. There isn't anything that can be ruled out as irrelevant to that effort of local adaptation, once we decide to make it. And it's only in your own life, in your own place, that the effort can be made.

. . . The ecological principle in agriculture . . . is to connect the genius of the place, to fit the farming to the farm."

Wendell Berry, poet-farmer

Meanwhile, feed the piglets in the top barn, install a pump to draw up waste water from the dairy onto the hill, consider the merits of installing a wind turbine, sell electricity from solar panels back to Ecotricity, endure the flat-lining of organic milk sales in the recession, characterise conventional farming as linear and organic as cyclical, give a talk to the Lyme Regis Society, follow the cows through a river of slurry to the milking shed, complete the Cattle Passports, select a suitable site on Higher Field for the next compost heap, move logs from the woodshed to the boiler house before the rain starts, cook the dinner and load and light the boiler. Then before bed, check nothing and no one has fallen into the slurry pit, check the birthing paddock, see if any cows are on heat or have escaped, look at the stars and the moon, curse the badgers and the foxes, shine a light into a fox's eyes and finally lie down in bed or, if necessary, on the kitchen couch.

Today dream the warm Chalk Sea:
clear, yet rich with clams
and Nautilus, starfish, sea-lilies
breathing and pluming,
giant lizards fanned by their tails
through the waves; and here
drowned – a flying pterosaur
who'd lost its way, bones still
delicate among the Foraminiferans
in the white Dorset lime,
those tiny millions loosed from
their calcareous chambered shells
(like grains of wheat) and blooms
of calcite crystal – Coccoliths –
once lit by the old Mesozoic sun.

In Sydling St Nicholas the air *'is cold and dry and, if we may judge from the congenity of the inhabitants, extremely salubrious.'* The village lies on Sydling Water, a tributary of the Frome River, at an altitude of 360 feet, the surrounding hills rising to 870 feet. In the Domesday Book it appears as Sidelince or Sydelince, from the Old English *sid* and *hlinc* ('broad ridge') and at that time comprised 54 households of villagers, smallholders and slaves, plough lands and meadow, pasture, woodland and 'mixed measures', with 3 watermills, 3 cob horses, 10 cattle and 250 sheep, 4 lord's plough teams and 14 men's plough teams. There are signs of Neolithic, Bronze and Iron Age settlements, Celtic field systems and Saxon strip lynchets on the chalk hills.

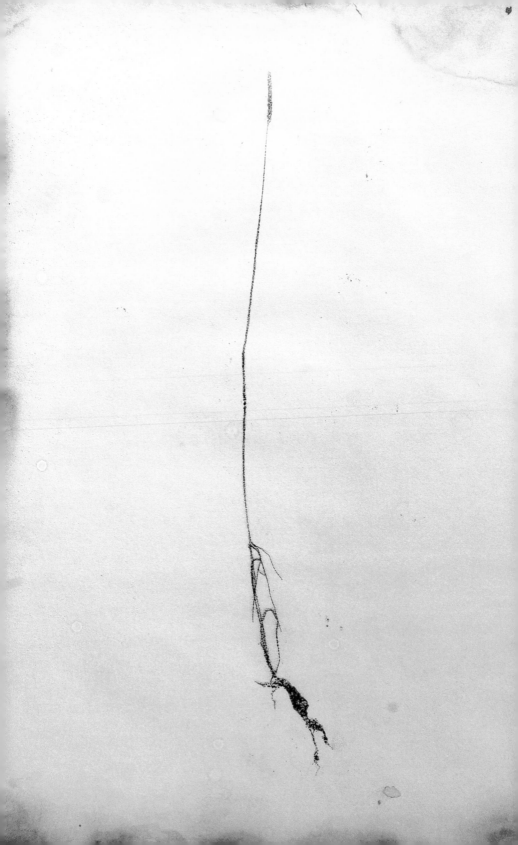

Huish Farm – *huis*, *hīwisc* Anglo-Saxon for self-sufficient dwelling or household; *uisg* water (Celtic). Start at Lower Combe, across Four Hills to Upper Coombe and The Hanging (a steep declivity), up to Huish Plantation and the Matsons with its Celtic field system, and Shearplace Hill (once Bronze Age timber round houses, enclosures, banks and ditches; Iron Age and Romano-British fields and trackways; signs of third- and fourth-century Roman reoccupation), Huish Barn, then Settlement, The Old Village, Hogslight, Top 50, Middle 50 and Bottom 50, Pond Bottom and the steep Giffords & Woodcock, Starveacre (or *Ranunculus arvensis*: corn buttercup, devil-on-all-sides, said to impoverish the soil or indicate a poor one), the Poorlots, where only church-goers could collect free wood on the way home from the service, and on to Reynard's Copse, Telstar, Bushes Barn with the new Forcey's Bell Tower and the cottages, Bushes Bottom and up to Colonel's, then all the way down to the water meadows (behind the cottages), flooded during the winter and grazed by sheep and cattle in the summer months.

Walk along the track to the sheep barn, find the farmer checking udders for damage or disease, his hands' knowledge as complex as his eyes'; walk with him to the chalk barn with its sheep pens and cattle shelter used by a nearby dairy farm; stride on with hair strewn and wet over Shearplace Hill and beyond, ghostly with Roman Legions marching on the ridge, ancient fertility rites, men hanged in the field called The Hanging, and on to Pond Bottom among the sheep, and past the rams towards Bushes Barn, where a grassy amphitheatre calls out for poets and song, and above, the headstones for Mother, and for Toby. Along to Bushes, and floating in the grass, the long white bath of Colonel Morris who was 6 feet 7 inches tall, and stories of the Forceys who lived in the old cottages, the children late to school for hiding in the bushes until all the curly-horned cows had passed by. Then back over to the farmhouse, past the silver horse, the hissing geese and the dog in the stream, to read a *Little Bit o' Nonsense about Sheep* by Henry Brewis, and find five new puppies in the garage and one black puppy lying in a coil of red hosepipe in the yard.

"November 28, 1.30pm – I'm up on the top of the hill. I've put my sheep onto what we call The Old Village and I'm now going to the field we call Poorlots where we've got two blue-faced Leicester rams out there with about eighty sheep. These two rams are virgins so I just want to make sure that everything's working all right as they've got eighty ewes to serve. I'll just see how they're getting on . . . Yeah, here I am out in the field, the rams seem to know what life's all about . . . and we've now come out into a 36-acre field which we call Colonel's, and again I've got three Beltex rams out here with 128 ewes, I think. Just gently walkng the rams and the ewes up to the top and hoping they'll form a nice little circle. It's all the start of life and hopefully, we will have them lambing in the middle of April."

John Morris, Huish Farm

To guide the sheep into the barn or a stall, bring your shoulders up gently, like a shrug, but with authority, keeping the arms wide and the hands as if in supplication. Be careful, because sheep can read emotional states in facial expressions, they're sensitive to noise and have a very strong sense of smell, with scent glands not only near their eyes but also between their toes. They have almost panoramic vision, can see behind themselves without turning their heads and can distinguish between black, red, brown, green, yellow and white. They can recognise and remember each other's faces and yours. If worked with quietly, patiently, they can even learn their own names.

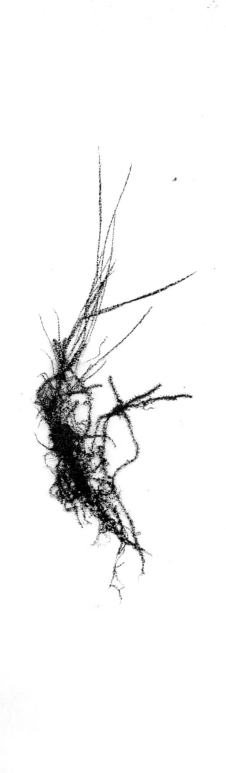

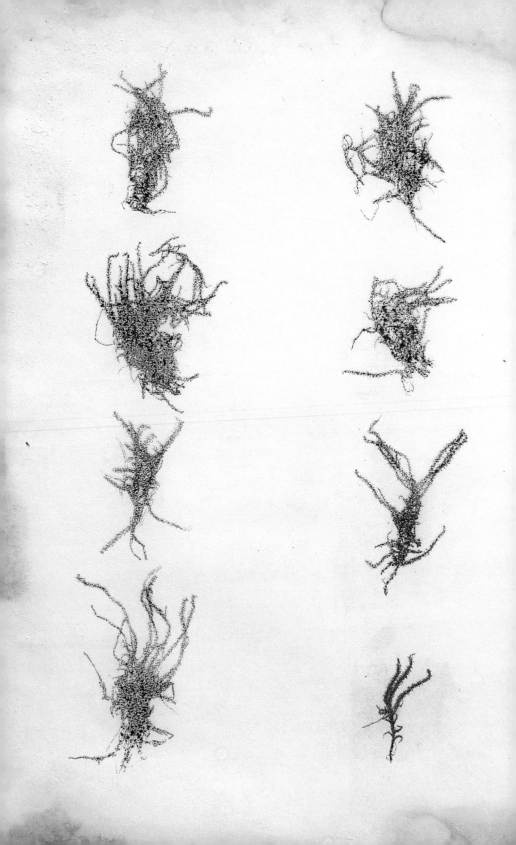

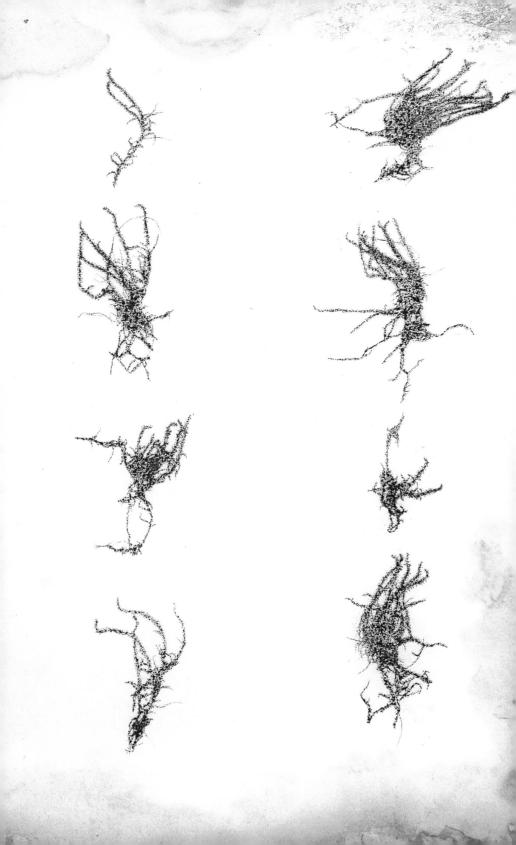

"I am walking down to my pond, dug in 1968–69, primarily as a fishing pond, and then my father had this great idea of planting poplar trees, which were all the rage then for matchsticks for Bryant & May, but as soon as he planted them they started to import poplar trees from Czechoslovakia; there was a great glut of poplar trees, nobody wanted them and so when I was 40 I had many of them cut down. But I've just gone and planted a load of willows for cricket bats for Gray-Nicholls, down on the water meadows, so I expect I shall be leaving the same thing for my sons William and Atticus – who'll ask 'what the hell do you do with all these willow-bat trees?' Trying to get the tree market right does seem to be impossible: you try and look twenty or thirty years in advance, plant when it's all the rage and then it seems to peter out, no market when they get to maturity, but that's life. Maybe William might do better, but you never know, maybe my willows will come into their own for cricket bats – William and Atticus might be batting at Lords for England, opening bat, both 99 not out, my willows in their bats and one brother running the other out . . ."

John Morris, Huish Farm

"December 4, four o'clock, and I've just finished doing my hedging all the way down to the pond and I've now seen why the water wasn't running in, it's all been blocked up at the trout farm with leaves and stuff so I've cleared all that so hopefully we'll get water flowing down to the pond. After my bit of hedging these last couple of days, my left hand has swelled up and so I think probably I've got a black-thorn in there but God knows, and also I seemed to have damaged a rib – I don't quite know how, though I know I had a fall and a stick went into my side and the doctor took one look at that and said ooh, that'll take six weeks to mend. Anyway, we are going to carry on with the challenges of another day – and I have just filled out a Movements Form which comes from DEFRA, the Department of Food and Rural Affairs, to say how many sheep I had on December 1. I think I wrote down 437, and how many lambs did I have plus rams and ewes that didn't go to the ram, and I wrote down 503. I hope that my numbers are right because if they aren't and I have an inspection from the Rural Payments Agency, I will get fined £3,000 – hopefully I am right, but we do live in fear of the RPA."

John Morris, Huish Farm

"I think it's Sunday 8 December, and what I'm doing today is I've got my sheepdog and we're rounding up some lambs now, we're going to put them in the yard down the bottom, and they're all going off to a dairy farm, because they've got better grass, and all the cows are in. They've got good grass which will fatten my lambs during the winter as I don't have grasses or stubble turnips or anything I can use. All my lambs plus some ewes that wouldn't have survived the winter on my sort of grass I send off to much better dairy leys, which are grown to produce lots of milk from their cows in Blackmore Vale – all good dairy grass, good dairy herds all down there and the farmers, they like the grass to be nibbled during the winter because it gives a better flush of grass in the spring; also that you're using fertiliser from the sheep – this is what the dairy farmers love, good grass early in the spring, all full of sugars and starches."

John Morris, Huish Farm

"Friday 13, it's a very dark, damp miserable day. I've got William up in the tractor and he's got his own seat and safety belt on; hopefully he can't go anywhere, and I'm going to take off my prong bucket and put on the grain bucket and William and I are going to pick up some logs that I chopped up the other day, and we're going to put them in the bucket. All a bit trial and error with lining up the buckets and moving the manure, all the horse manure from the stables and I have a stubble field going into rape in August and I can just spread this horse manure out on the stubble ground now to give it a bit more nitrogen in the spring – *hey, we're making art, William, we're making a shape with our manure . . .*"

John Morris, Huish Farm

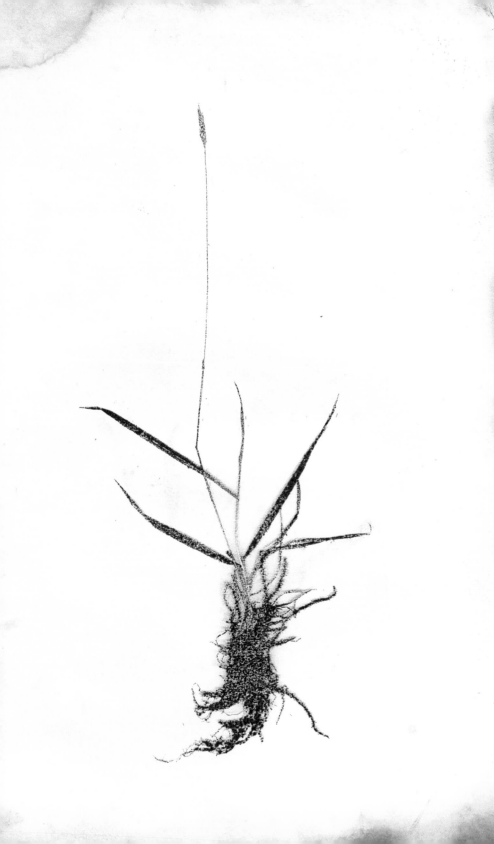

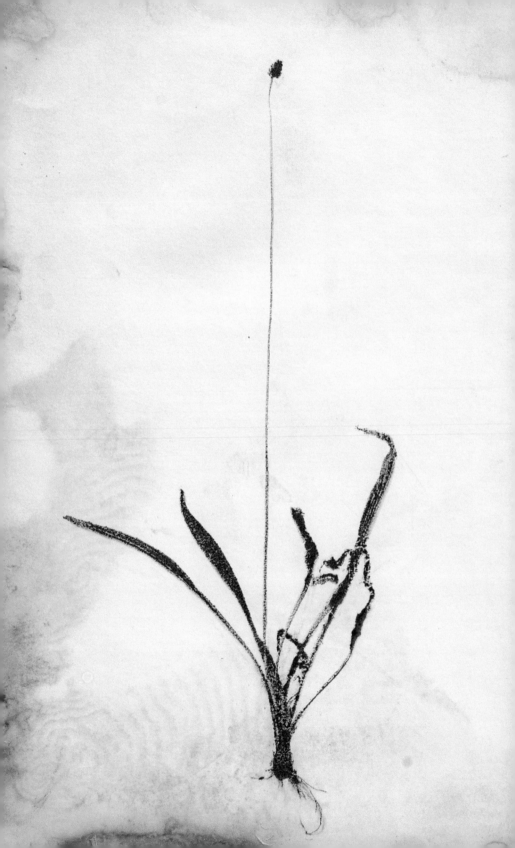

"Here we are now back underneath Bulbarrow with another load of lambs, got a very nasty corner to take and it really is in deepest, darkest Dorset, the little country lanes, hedges everywhere, oak trees, ash, hazel, very very wet ground down through here, sort of had a wet winter down here, the whole place is absolutely flooded but the grass is still very very green, whilst back at home the grass has turned brown and through here it's as green as anything, you know, and you just get the odd house here and there and the odd hamlet. My lambs will be very happy, nice and sheltered all down here and if it snows they can shelter underneath the hedges, they won't be exposed up on our downland, no – lovely. I've taken over 206 lambs to the Miller Farm in the heart of the Blackmore Vale and these will all now get fattened, they'll stay on this lovely lush grass hopefully for a couple of months and the lambs will fatten here on the grass and also I brought 70 ewes that I decided not to put to the ram, I didn't think they would survive another winter at Huish Farm."

John Morris, Huish Farm

Clean out the sheep trailer, stop cleaning the trailer when Wessex Water come round looking for leaks, visit the Accountant, watch the corn and winter oilseed rape keep on growing after a very long wet mild winter, spread the fertiliser when the land is dry enough to take the weight of the machines, maintain the lambing yard, the sheep pens, the barns, the grain store, stables, farmhouse, machinery, pasture, arable fields, Higher Stewardship Level margins, fences, the hedges, paths, tracks, stiles, family, sheep, horses, pheasants and partridges; seat ten women from the local WI on the charabanc and tow them with a tractor around the farm in beautiful evening light, sit in the bath outside Bushes Barn with some cans of beer watching the marathon runners on the ridge; plough, sow, wait, harvest, plough, sow, wait, harvest; produce food for the nation.

Apply the terms of the ten-year Higher Level Stewardship scheme for Natural England, who will pay you to make a bridle gate, dog gate, timber stile or kissing gate, to manage your hedgerows and ancient trees, reduce soil erosion and run off, to restore your water meadows, ponds, stone walls and earth banks, and to pay attention to the height of your swards and your tussocks. Then give over 30 hectares to long-overwintered stubble and two hectares for the corn buntings (mustard, spring wheat, barley, white or red millet and triticale); sow millet, barley, quinoa and kale at the margins of your fields to help *Bring back the Arable Six* – the grey partridge, yellow wagtail, lapwing, tree sparrow, corn bunting and turtle dove – and grow nectar-rich red clover, alsike clover, wild marjoram, bird's-foot trefoil, sanfoin, musk mallow and knapweed, for the bees in the summer.

Observe that sheep use both their lips and tongues to select grass, and that they have a split in their upper lip enabling them to pick off the parts of the plant they prefer, which are those easier to digest and the most nutritious. Like cows, they don't have top front teeth so they chew against a thick pad in the top of their mouths. It has been reported that sheep can be effective for conservation grazing, and that grazing lambs can be as good as herbicides in the control of weeds, and with alfalfa, for example, they can control insects as successfully as insecticides.

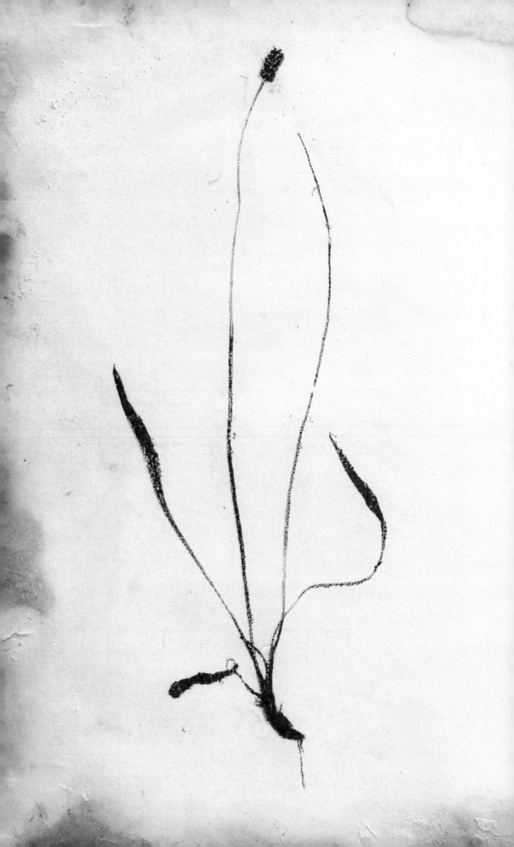

The Bell Tower

I saw the tower first through leaves at the corner of Ram's
Plot on Manor Farm, saw the tower again from the stile
at the edge of the wood where the stone sculptures stand
(five cherry trees, twenty beech) and it gave me direction,

called my eye to glide over the sweep of grass and sand-
fields to a single point. Arriving, I circled this alone tower,
this lonely cone rising up by Forcey's tree and three white
baths below the ruined cottages (fireplaces, rusting pans

exposed), by the barn stacked full with blue desks, an owl
or a pigeon or perhaps a long-lost turtle-dove in the rafters.
I sat inside the tower, feet far off the ground, I was a child,
looking to the right at a land and sky contained, precious,

and quickly I looked to the left and again to the right to see
this strip once more defined and then I rang the bell, loud,
strong, sharp. Who heard that bell, I asked, how should
or could they answer? And I looked up into the bell's eye,

heard again its beat, felt our own vain and lonely calling
in the valley of the fields, heard by a pigeon, owl or turtle-
dove, by the silent blue-faced sheep, the cows in Dollens'
meadows or two roe deer (their tidy leaping), and I cried.

"Indoor lambing? No! The price of straw and the antibiotics, water and mud – you need so much help, moving them about, indoor pen, outdoor pen, transport boxes out to the fields. If it's fine weather and the predators are kept away, it works. Two years ago I should have just stayed in bed for ten days . . . But this is the most natural way of doing it. Here are these black rams, blue-faced Leicesters with the Scotties. They don't like the cold weather. Nor the wet – we had a wet autumn and the rams wouldn't work in the rain – they won't do anything unless it's right. *Ah, you want VIP treatment, go on, go on.* Birth, it's a very rare thing to see. I must put a dot on that lamb's head, but not yet, need to leave it alone (74, *number 74*) for a bit. OK, on we go, hah, brilliant. She hasn't got a prolapse. Always the problem of the lambs getting muddled up. *Oh, well done, old girl.* Number 90. *Well done, girls!* This is more like it. It's all happening out here. *What number are you – 91!*"

John Morris, Huish Farm

"I woke up today at 4 am to John's agony with cramp. I put a load of washing on and a load of drying in and a swift tidy of the kitchen following an unruly lunch party the day before. Then I crept back to bed until six when the boys awoke and John had already left to do the sheep. I dressed the two children, fed them and cleared up. I measured up and scored lines for the new CCTV we are installing and ordered more cable. Put another load on. Spoke to a building company about a sewage matter, fed the horse, jump-started the Kubota, planted four rows of lettuce and two rows of sweet pea and played with the boys. Mowed the lawn and went to a point-to-point at Seaborough where I spoke to everyone I needed to in order to keep farmerly relations alive, returned via Yeovil to collect John's dry cleaning and buy fruit and stopped off to have a quick snack with Mother; arrived home, did more washing, tidied the kitchen, called a friend, played with the puppy, sat John down and told him his diary for the month, cooked supper, tidied up after it, did the accounts of the cottages, fixed a saucepan handle, fixed a broken slat on the garden parasol, fed the horse and . . . this is beginning to feel like a very complicated palindrome . . ."

S-J Morris, Huish Farm

We're driving over the fields,
Hogslight up to Starveacre,
it's 6 am and we're checking
the pregnant ewes and the lambs,
we sweep up and round and down
and in Bottom 50, the farmer gathers up
a lost newborn lamb and places it
between my feet in the heated footwell
of the Land Rover until we can reach the barn,
then we're in Top 50 and he's out of
the jeep again, with the sheepdog, Scally,
racing after and bearing to the ground
a ewe with a prolapse (bright red)
and while he's fitting the prolapse
harness, Scally, butted unconscious
by a ram last month, leaps on to my lap
and leans hard into my chest, panting
and trembling, her heart beating
right up against mine.

"*N*ow *then, now then, now then.* Something
not quite right with this one (the one with the big
head) . . . I'm always very reluctant to bring them
in, unless they're going to die. *Marvellous, right,
everyone stay where you are.* I've got thirteen
new sheep and they're late lambers – why? The
scanner tells me they're all in lamb, I wait with
baited breath. Hope they don't all lamb in the
same forty-eight hours. There's Atticus, a black-
faced ewe, with two lambs – they were in a funny
old position, on their sides, they weren't dropping
down. If a lamb has an ear up, it's all right.
Occasionally they'll catch you by surprise. *Hallo
old girl.* There we are, a drive-by birth – I've now
seen two in two days. That terrible year, I had one
sheep I had to catch, didn't catch it and it went
all the way down – I picked up a dozen lambs the
next morning, they'd got all mixed up and lost
their mums and froze to death. Just the nature of
the beast, outdoor, my way of doing it."

John Morris, Huish Farm

"Going round another mob of sheep and the lambs and then what I want to do is get my tractor up with the bucket on and load up these logs, but I've got to pick William up at 2.30 – by the time I've done the sheep I don't expect I'll have the chance to do it, but hopefully on Sunday, my rib will be a lot better. OK, sorry to be moaning but it's very windy up here, the sun's out, we can see all round, can see Hardy's monument, it's just a fantastic office for working up here, not a soul, the only thing you can hear is the wind. I'm incredibly lucky in what I do in my life and I hope that I'll keep repeating that over and over again."

John Morris, Huish Farm

"I was soon passing our farmyard, which adjoined the road. There it was, deserted, silent, a pocket of gloom, a nonentity of a place, something to pass by. Was it really possible, I asked myself, that this slushy yard, so humble, so lacking in all the props and appointments of Power, was yet the foundation of society? Yet so it was. Upon this the fabric rested, upon this was erected all that glittered and all that shone; and I knew that the lighted palace from which I had come where the Figures paced on the polished floor, and the Magicians emerged with food from behind the screens, could not otherwise exist at all. I got off my bicycle and gazed into the farmyard – at the stable door, the pile of manure, the muddy pool, the old binder in the corner, the oil-cans and sacks, the three wagons and the two carts under the shelter. I peered at these things through the dreary dank of the dripping darkness, with some intensity, as if aware that here only, in this place, and in such guise, could I find the roots of grandeur and the keys of life."

John Stewart Collis,
The Worm Forgives the Plough

"Imagine an infinite sea of energy filling empty space, with waves moving around in there, occasionally coming together and producing an intense pulse. Let's say one particular pulse comes together and expands, creating our universe of space–time and matter. But there could well be other such pulses. To us, that pulse looks like a big bang; in a greater context, it's a little ripple. Everything emerges by unfoldment from the holomovement, then enfolds back into the implicate order. I call the enfolding process "implicating," and the unfolding "explicating." The implicate and explicate together are a flowing, undivided wholeness. Every part of the universe is related to every other part but in different degrees."

David Bohm, Physicist

Below the rising meadow-grass
(narrow leaves as fine as pins)
another mass of tangled moss:
Mougeot's Yoke or Polytrichum
Commune (Hair Cap), just like
Strictum, growing fast in warm
Antartica. And this one's loosed
its water-hold of moss – a lone
white flower, Meadow Saxifrage –
and Bird's-foot Trefoil sings
its long-root song, known
round here as Eggs-and-Bacon
or Tom Thumb's Fingers-and-
Thumbs, a crown of yellow
slippers edged or lined with red.

Bos taurus (cow) is a terrestrial artiodactyl,
a mammal whose hoofs conceal four toes,
of which the third and fourth bear
the weight equally.

This even-toed ungulate evolved from
the great wild auroch (ox) in the Near East
(now Iran) about 10,500 years ago;
the last auroch died in 1627 in Poland.

80% of the genes of cows and humans
are the same, with cows being more like humans
in their chromosomal make up
than are rats and mice.

Turn right at Dollens farmhouse, cowsheds and haybarns into Lower Dairy, through flourishing clover and up into Higher Dairy (where this paper was buried). Climb up through Steeps, higher still to Peak End, across into Yew Tree, down into Higher Church and Church Meadows, see the cows at the water trough, on down to Maize Ground and back past the farmhouse and the barns. Cross the lane for Big Croad (or chicken), Little Croad, Corn Ground and Cattens (or Battens, who once lived there), then behind the houses, more pasture: East Field, Dock Plot and City Meadows (perhaps the old city of the poor) or further up to Curden, Pescombe (common family name) and Fred Marshes (previous owner), then up into Rough Hill or down to Zephyrs (last owned by the Millers who loved to sail the Greek Islands – feel that sea breeze) and Inland Revenue (not what you're thinking). Then Huish, Huish 10, across to Saxons (settlement beyond the hedge) or left for 3 in 1 or up to Clovers and the undulating Humpty. Yet further to 3 Corners and Hill Pits (dug for flint) and Hill Barn, to look in on the youngstock, and left up to 100 Acres South and 100 Acres North, Crown Point (an SSSI, close to where the cubit of turf was taken for this book) and Crown Cap, which from afar looks scalloped like a crown. Then below, Sidelines, Hands Hole, Pond Hill and George's Knap (previous owner) and above, Yonder 10 Acres and Charities, which is stony and no good at all.

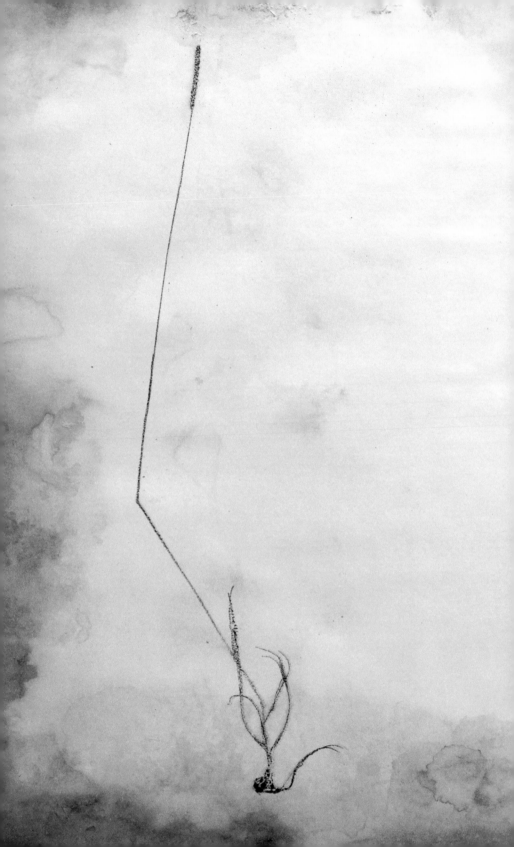

This is the genealogy of the cows at Dollens Farm:
120 original names, given by Chris Legg's father –
now 24. It's a closed herd, immune to many viruses.

Abbis (10) Agatha Alison **Alma** (23) **Amy** (6) Anne
Anita Aster Audrey Avril Ays **Bandy** (2) Beau Beauty
Bella Belle Beryl **Betty** (7) **Blackbird** (37) Blackjack
Blacky Bloom Blossom Bluebell Bluebird Bomber
Bridget **Bristle** (28) Brownie Buttercup **Camilla** (5)
Candy Caroline Catherine Charm Cherry Chestnut
Christobel Christine Clover Companula Connie
Coomb Cosmo Coco Coconut Cola **Colleen** (5)
Cora (7) Crystal **Cuckoo** (11) Daffodil Daisy
Damson (2) Dandy Daphne Darkie Dinky **Dorcas**
(4) **Doreen** (40) Doris Dot Duchesse Dulcie Ecila Ella
Emma **Ena** (1) Edna Ethel Emerald Fanny Foxglove
Flossie (49) Freda Gay **Georgina** (2) Gerie Gertie
Gladys Graceful Greta Grizzle **Gwen** (7) Gwenda
Honey Ivy Jane **Joy** (9) June Knott Lalina Lemon
Lofty Magpie Manila Marigold Mayflower Moppit
Myrlie Nina Queen Panda Pansy Pat **Phyliss** (2)
Polly (3) Rowena Sally Sarah Silver Soo Spot Stumpy
Sue **Susan** (7) **Trudi** (8) **Winnie** (14) and Winter

(S.A. Legg & Sons)

Get up at 3.30 am for the 5 am milking, five days a week. Shut the cows in the collecting yard, check all the cows in the maternity yards, clean the yards with the scraper tractor, put new supplies of silage in the feeder trailers, milk 170 cows, first wiping each cow's udders with a paper towel before attaching the milking machine. Afterwards, dip each teat in glycerine and iodine, wash down the milking parlour, welcome the workforce (it's 7 am by now), feed 150 youngstock, let out the hens, read the rain guage for the Met Office, check for bulling cows and the maternity cows, check the cows' rationing on the dairy computer, help Doreen to give birth to a second twin, check the post, supervise hedge trimming and dung-heaping, clean out the covered lying areas, arrange the servicing of the dirty-water system, patch up new grass leys suffering from slow germination, and get permission from the Soil Association to apply slug pellets.

Count the number of Friesian heifer calves (it's 46) and anticipate another 79 calves. Collect wood for the renewable fuel biomass boiler; store and dry the wood for a year. Bring in all the cattle except for the Aberdeen Angus, allow the dairy cows a choice of staying in or out at night, observing their preference for lying in the barns. Shut the cows in the yard, clean the yards, fill the silage trailers again and start the afternoon milking at 2.30pm. Then move straw, ensure Doreen's calves have had colostrum, phone the AI man, pay the bills and wages, run the village Post Office from home every Thursday, go to the vet's, drive down country lanes to the middle of nowhere to get a spare part, respond to the demands of the weather, keep on top of the gardening, enrich the soil, admire the proliferation of flora and fauna and the return of unusual birds and butterflies, look out of the windows and be thankful.

Later, notice the swallows residing in the biomass fuel boiler and then wait for the swallows to fledge; only then blow a new load of pellets into the boiler store. Meanwhile, witness the stray pheasants in the hen paddock and apprehend the coming of autumn. Later, dig out twelve inches of mud along the track from field to dairy, lay a stone mixture topped with oolitic limestone, replace safety covers on the dirty-water system, install new ventilated capped covers for the covered barns, clear the guttering and the drainpipes and observe new rules regarding slurry. Put a roof on the collecting yard to meet new laws, serve the heifers with mixed-sex semen, clean out the calf house and cancel the Harvest Festival celebrations in the yard due to bad weather.

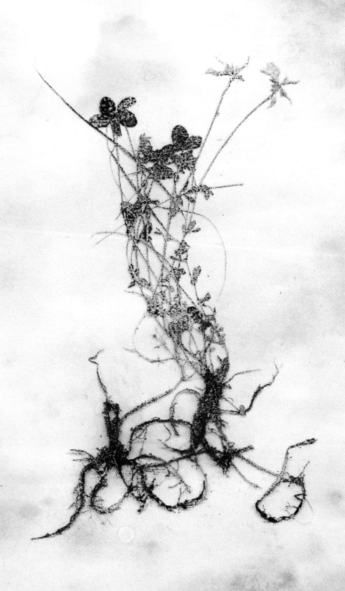

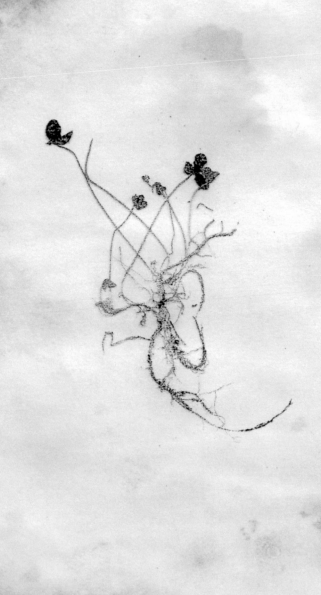

Endure six weeks of rain, watch the springs bubbling and secondary springs flowing. Abandon normal winter jobs but continue cleaning out the covered yards and the winter-housing barns. Clear the roofs and drains and milk the cows in a foot of flood water. Note the similarities in character between the Angus bulls. Watch The General tossing his head in the air and bellowing loudly; discover The General hiding in the woods two nights running. Later, read the pregnancy diagnosis test (70 cows are in calf) and calculate how much silage will be needed. Compare the prices of conventional and organic seed corn and meet the agronomist who will take a sample of the corn. Clean and sow the farm's own barley seed, use a bush whacker to cut avenues through the gorse and watch the natural grassland and wild flowers regenerate.

"My decision to become an organic farmer took shape over a period of years with many different events and thoughts coming together. Suzanne and I were becoming increasingly concerned about the amount and cost of sprays and fertilisers we were using and were beginning to ask is this 'right'? I was fast approaching 50 and was feeling that we were running faster and faster only to stand still! Around this time Sydling Farms decided to become organic and I started to watch what was happening with great interest. It soon became apparent to me that it didn't matter how good your soil was if you couldn't grow clover, which fortunately we can. So I approached the Soil Association and an advisor took us to see Will Best [at Manor Farm] who was very much a pioneer in the organic movement . . . The more I discussed the subject, the ideas of mixed farming, self-sufficiency and sustainability became more and more appealing. Our farm has a large area of SSSI which I have always enjoyed and farming organically is so much more nature-friendly that it just seemed a perfect fit."

Chris Legg, Dollens Farm

Moschatel
Nodding Bur-marigold
Trifid Bur-marigold
Sneezewort
Hautbois Strawberry
Dense-flowered Fumitory
Three-cornered Garlic
Marsh Foxtail
Pyramidal Orchid
Pearly Everlasting
Balkan Anemone
Stinking Chamomile
Loose Silky-bent
Parsley-piert
Fool's-water-cress
Hairy Rock-cress
Opposite-leaved Golden Saxifrage
Greater Quaking-grass
(*Dorset name*, Wagwanton)
Italian Lords-and-Ladies
Black Horehound
Confused Michaelmas
Lesser Water-parsnip
Chimney Bellflower
Hairy Bitter-cress
Cuckooflower
Canadian Fleabane
New Zealand Pigmyweed
Beaked Hawk's-beard
Dodder
Sowbread
Indian-rhubarb
Musk Storks-bill
Corncockle
Dove's foot Crane's-bill
Pencilled Crane's-bill
Eastern Gladiolus
Corsican Hellebore
Yorkshire-fog
Shaggy Soldier
Mousetailplant
Corky-fruited Water-dropwort
Petty Whin
Rose-of-Sharon

Perforate St John's-wort
Cat's-ear
Ploughman's spikenard
Toad Rush
Round-leaved Fluellen
Henbit Dead-nettle
American Skunk-cabbage
Bladdernut
Abraham-Isaac-Jacob
Zigzag Clover
Navelwort
(*Dorset name* Cups-and-saucers)
Moth Mullein
Narcissus poeticus
Sticky Mouse-ear
Good-King-Henry
Fig-leaved Goosefoot
Common Blue-sow-thistle
Autumn Ladies'-tresses
Pendulous Sedge
Twayblade
Spiny Restharrow
Pellitory-of-the-wall
Marsh Lousewort
Amphibious Bistort
Butterbur
Timothy
Purple Toadflax
Fairy Flax
Rat's tail-Fescue
Bristly Oxtongue
Mouse-ear-hawkweed
Lesser Butterfly-orchid
Trailing Tormentil
Yellow Corydalis
Goldilocks Buttercup
Monk's-hood
Buffalo-bur
Mind-your-own-business
Flea Sedge
Purple Toothwort
Tutsan
Venus's-looking-glass
Narcissus pseudonarcissus

"The hay
Smelt of how
The sky loved the earth [. . .]"

John Berger, from 'Old Love Poem'

Here's sweet vernal grass, meadowsweet, the
fescues; sainfoin on dry gound, timothy on heavy
land. The protein in clover is mainly in the stems;
grazing thickens the crop, and you can cut the hay
later, so the skylarks can nest.

Caring without cease for the land

"Even before Chris and I were married in 1979, Mrs Legg (my mother-in-law) very kindly allowed me to take over the farm records, accounts and wages. I was thrilled; numbers, figures, sums, accurate records and dates, I just love. Over the years we have modernised and no longer are our accounts hand-written in the enormous 'Guildhall Cash Analysis Book'! Farm accounts and wages, although important, is a very unnoticed job, unpaid and always in the background. It is for the farmer essential but not essential in his daily routine. That was in the past. It is now so important, to survive, to take an active interest in the financial side of the business. I always analyse and question expenditure. I asked irritating questions, and more and more I was asking 'Why are we spending so much money on sprays and fertilisers, what are the benefits, what profit are we making from the crops, why are our contractors' bills so high, why don't we concentrate on what we're good at – dairy farming?' And so the seed was sown. The conventional farmers ridiculed Chris, the old farmers thought he was crazy, but in 2007 the decision was made to farm organically."

Suzanne Legg, Dollens Farm

"The post-war years encouraged farmers to improve the land by using artificial fertilisers and chemical sprays. In the relatively short time of being an organic farmer, we have seen, contrary to previous belief, how drastically our soil has been enriched and improved, how the wildlife, plants, flora, unusual birds and butterlies have all increased significantly in numbers. I hope that future generations of farmers will realise what damage we have done, unknowingly, to our environment. We have been a very wasteful world; we must try to make amends for the damage we have done to this earth. The Legg family have been farming in Dorset for at least seven generations – all dairy farmers, as far back as the mid-1700s. In this tiny part of the world, known as Sydling St Nicholas, I hope future generations will continue farming and embody the principles and ethos of organic farming – we are just custodians of the land for future generations."

Suzanne Legg, Dollens Farm

"I have always felt very 'connected' to the land and if anything farming organically has made an even stronger bond. Organic farming is proactive farming and by that I mean you have to anticipate problems and plan in much more detail for all eventualities; the values that have developed are to work with Nature – not to try to conquer it, because Nature will always win! I believe strongly in mixed farming, which is really a system of recycling in which all aspects of the farm are interdependent and reliant on one another. Organic farming and Nature go hand in hand and we have seen an increase in bird life on the farm. I would say to future generations, enjoy farming, work with Nature, and like the American Indians, respect your land, because it all starts with a healthy soil."

Chris Legg, Dollens Farm

"Albert Howard, in the middle of the last century, said that if you want to know how to farm, you must look at the forest. Learn what nature does. You've got to imitate her methods. She always keeps the ground covered. She always farms with animals. She maintains the highest possible diversity of plants and animals. She wastes nothing. She maintains large reserves of fertility. She leaves, then, her crops to defend themselves against pests and diseases."

Wendell Berry

Where is Gwen or Bristle or Trudi in the queue for the milking? It's the same every time except for Dorcas who always decides her position at the last minute. Which cow is blearing? Cows are sensitive, they like order, their tongues are long and pink and if they trust you they will lick you. When they're let out in spring they skip and leap, even though they weigh three quarters of a ton. You can immunise your calves against red tick by exposing them to a few of those ticks; it's the same with midges. The heifers are in season every 21 days, the bull is hiding and the cock is crowing and there's drizzle and mist over the milking shed this morning. A 'night out' for the dairy farmer is a trip up the hill on the quad bike in the gloaming.

I OO leaves of 300 gsm Snowden cartridge paper were buried in Lower Dairy field on Dollens Farm and left in the ground for ten months.

A square cubit of turf, with its green fronds and yellow flowers waving in the early summer breeze, was lifted from another Dollens field.

The paper was dug from the ground – changed by time, minerals, moisture, enzymes. The sheaves were then soaked, gently separated and pegged up to dry.

Sixty clumps or single plants from the square cubit of turf were scanned flat and printed directly on to acetate, then transferred to the paper while the ink was still wet.

References

'*across the talking corn she goes*' is taken from Emily Dickinson's poem 'An English Breeze'.

'*corn was threshed with flails . . .*' is taken from an online article by Will Best about Godmanstone.

'*I come into the peace of wild things*' is taken from Wendell Berry's poem 'The Peace of Wild Things'.

Philip Hansford & Tony Pinkus, *The Herdsman's Introduction to Homeopathy* (1998).

'*The thresher is a machine which certainly holds the attention . . .*' was the observation of John Stewart Collis in *The Worm Forgives the Plough* (1946/7).

Descriptions of Godmanstone and Sydling are taken or adapted from Hutchin's *General View of the Agriculture of the County of Dorset* (1812) and the Domesday Book [online].

The poem 'I saw the tower first through leaves' was written for the unveiling of Guy Martin's Forcey's Tower, 4 October 2014.

The Wendell Berry quotations come from an interview with the poet by Jim Leach, Chair of the National Endowment for the Humanities, 2012. Berry quotes Albert Howard in the same interview.

'*caring without cease for the land*' comes from L.P. Wilkinson's 1982 introduction to Virgil's *Georgics* (*c.*36–29BC), in which the poet passionately advocates 'caring without cease' for the land and for the crops and animals it sustained.

David Bohm, interviewed by F. David Peat and John Briggs, originally published in *Omni*, January 1987.

Acknowledgements

This work could not have been made without the generosity, time and information offered by the farmers at Manor Farm, Huish Farm and Dollens Farm. We would like to thank Will and Pam Best, John and S-J Morris, and Chris and Suzanne Legg.

Thanks are also due to Philip Hansford, formerly herdsman at Manor Farm.

The artists were commissioned in 2013–14 to make a series of artworks inspired by the work of the three farms by Cape Farewell, a cultural organisation concerned with climate change. Special thanks are due to the Director of Cape Farewell, David Buckland, and also to Marente van der Valk and Yasmine Ostendorf.

Published by Cape Farewell & Little Toller Books in 2015

Text © Kay Syrad 2015
Jacket and internal illustrations © Chris Drury 2015

The right of Kay Syrad and Chris Drury to be identified as the authors of this work has been asserted by them in accordance with Copyright, Design and Patents Act 1988

Typeset in Sabon by Little Toller Books

Printed in Navarre, Spain

All papers used by Cape Farewell and Little Toller Books are natural, recyclable products made from wood grown in sustainable, well-managed forests

A catalogue record for this book is available from the British Library

ISBN 978-1-908213-34-1

Little Toller Books, Lower Dairy, Toller Fratrum, Dorset DT2 OEL
www.littletoller.co.uk

Cape Farewell, University of the Arts London, Chelsea College of Arts,
16 John Islip Street, London SW1 4JU
www.capefarewell.com